TRIUMPH

CLASSIC MOTORCYCLES
TRIUMPH

DON MORLEY

OSPREY
AUTOMOTIVE

Thanks are due, as always, to those who helped compile this project, and no one deserves more credit than the many fellow Vintage Motor Cycle Club members who so generously allowed me to photogrqph their beloved machines.

Grateful thanks also go to Alan Williams of the Imperial War Museum, along with Gladys Jones and my old friend Nick Nicholls, each of whom raided their own photo files to fill in some of the remaining gaps.

Joy Emerson deserves a particular mention, both for sorting out my spelling and meticulously typing the manuscript, and finally Nicholas Collins and Ian Penberthy of Osprey, without whose help I wouldn't even have started. Thank you all.

Don Morley
June 1990

Published in 1991 by Osprey an imprint of
Reed Consumer Books Limited
Michelin House, 81 Fulham Road, London SW3 6RB
Reprinted 1994

British Library Catalouging in Publication Data
Morley, Don
   Triumph.
   1. British motorcycles, history
   I. Title II. Series
   629.22750941
ISBN 1–85532–124–6
Editor Ian Penberthy
Page design Angela Posen
Printed and bound in Hong Kong
Produced by Mandarin Offset

Front cover
Ray Knight aboard the 490 cc RSM/Triumph during an Isle of Man foray

Page 1
Triumph's 1970 Bonneville – best of them all in the author's opinion

Right
1920s Coventry and a four-valve Ricardo with Gloria sidecar

For a catalogue of all books published by Osprey Automotive please write to:

The Marketing Manager, Consumer Catalogue Department
Osprey Publishing, Reed Consumer Books Limited, Michelin House
81 Fulham Road, London SW3 6RB

Contents

Introduction

I make no apologies for mentioning Edward Turner many times within the coming pages, for whilst others came and went during Meriden's most vital years between 1935 and 1967, he WAS Triumph. Not one design ever escaped the once great factory without his indelible stamp.

E.T., as he popularly (and occasionally unpopularly) became known, variously held the managing director's, chief executive's, and Chairman's roles, whilst always autocratically holding on to the reins as chief designer. He brought to the company a single-minded strength which, ironically, eventually became its greatest weakness.

Many stories abound from former Triumph employees as to how E.T. could be tyrannical, egotistical, arrogant, hot-headed, overbearing, unjust and then charming, all within a matter of minutes. Yet he was respected by most and, indeed, even worshipped for his rare breed of inspirational genius.

Those who made a habit of standing up to the great man tended to be fired often and then later reinstated, but this was a risky business. The wisest among them learned to survive longest by doing the job precisely how E.T. wanted it done, or at least until his back was turned! This became almost established practice which, in turn, saved the reputation of more than one Triumph product, for occasionally E.T. had an unfortunate tendency to produce flimsy designs. However, he

TRIUMPH

The Best Motorcycle in the World

P. H. ALVES—A.C.U. Trials Champion and four times member of winning British ??? in the International ??? Days Trial.

Above
*A works prototype overhead-cam Fury,
whose unsuccessful development virtually
bankrupted the parent BSA company*

Left
*A silhouette of Brian Relph's totally
original 1954 Tiger 110, surely THE
archetypal Turner Triumph*

Opposite page
*Turner's Triumphs were arguably the
best looking and usually well engineered,
although it took another couple of decades
beyond this advert's claim and Doug
Hele's skills before they handled to match*

would blow a gasket should anyone, even Bert Hopwood, his long-suffering number two, dare to point out any weaknesses.

Hopwood and Co. did what they could to quietly strengthen or modify, with perhaps even the master's knowing, but unstated, approval, as long as there had not been any face-to-face conflict. However, Triumph's pre-1963 motorcycles lost out in the meantime because of their almost traditionally weak chassis. Not that Turner's models ever handled really badly prior to that point, but they certainly weren't top bracket until after E.T.'s retirement when Messrs Doug Hele and Hopwood could put matters right at last.

Turner's involvement didn't end there, however, for he continued as a director and accepted overall responsibility for future product designs. This was when he foisted his desperately under-engineered 350 cc ohc Bandit/Fury models on to BSA's weak management who really should have known a little better. BSA/Triumph faced an £8 million loss and a takeover situation by the time they gave up trying to sort the bugs from those bikes.

Edward Turner himself finally passed away in 1973 at his Dorking home (not six miles away from where this manuscript was written), almost at the very moment that Triumph's employees were organizing their long sit-in.

So much of Triumph's history had evolved around this single, and at times Churchillian, genius, who sadly stayed on in the job for just a little too long.

Teutonic beginnings

Siegfried Bettmann set off for England, in search of fame and fortune, at almost the moment when his compatriots, Daimler and Maybach, began constructing the world's first motorized two-wheeler in Germany. Unlike them, however, he was not an engineer, and his two-wheel interests would, as yet, be confined to pedalling around London in search of a job.

Bettman had been a language student and, in addition to his native German, he spoke fluent French and English, making him an ideal choice when he finally found employment with a firm called Kelly's during 1884. Kelly's were (and still are) international map and street directory publishers, and his new role would be to sell display advertising to their numerous clients abroad.

A serious policy disagreement at Kelly's prompted him to leave a year later

Below
Built during 1912 and used by just three owners from new, John Richardson's unrestored $3\frac{1}{2}$ hp is totally original

and set up in business as an export/import agent, acting on behalf of various German- and British-based trading companies. He also commenced buying British-built pedal bicycles to sell under his own brand name in Germany.

The bicycles were all made by William Andrews of Birmingham, and were merely re-badged for export with the Bettman & Co. name. However, the firm's founder soon realized that he needed a catchier and more internationally acceptable brand name to stand any hope of expanding his business much further. He chose 'Triumph' during 1886, partly because it seemed to have just the right sort of extrovert ring, but primarily as it enjoyed precisely the same meaning in most other languages. The new Triumph brand products would still be bought in exactly as before, however.

Meanwhile, a German engineer named Mauritz Johann Schulte also set out for London during 1887. Soon after, he joined Bettmann, not only as his new junior partner, but also as the company's first trained engineer. It was he who persuaded Bettmann that business could be even better if they were seen both to make and market their products.

Coventry was chosen instead of London for their new headquarters, simply because it lay more centrally to the available skills of Britain's industrial heartland. So it was that Triumph and Coventry became almost synonymous for the best part of a century, the 1889-onwards two-wheeler dynasty operating from a factory sited right in this proud city's centre.

The year 1902 brought the company's first motorcycle, which was powered by a Belgian Minerva engine, and Orial-TWN (Triumph Germany) commenced producing much the same range from a factory in Nüremberg a year later. (That operation was sold off again during the Depression of the late 1920s and then continued independently as TWN Motorcycles until 1957, when they were finally bought out and closed down by the electrical giants Grundig.)

Triumph's first motorcycle to be powered by their own engine was the 3 hp model, which had arrived by 1905. In 1908 Jack Marshall gave them their first win in a TT race when he beat the more fancied Matchless ridden by its manufacturer Charlie Collier. In doing so, he put up a new 42.08 mph record speed lap, bringing in even more orders for similar machines.

Meanwhile, Bettmann had become a much respected local politician and, despite being a German in England at a time when war was looming, found himself elected as Mayor of Coventry from 1913 to 1914. Schulte also stayed on in the UK to work on his new 225 cc two-stroke Junior model and a prototype vertical twin.

Unfortunately, the latter engine proved uneconomical to produce, so Triumph would have to wait another 20 years or so for the arrival of designer Val Page before the company reached what would prove to be its real metamorphosis. In the meantime, however, Schulte did come up with the famous model H (4 hp) which, at the time, became Triumph's best ever seller.

One of the period's best known motorcycling writers visited the Marne during 1914, soon after the model H's military début for a first-hand look at how motorcycles were coping with the muddy battlefields of Flanders. Under the pseudonym 'Kucklos', he reported of meeting '24 khaki boys of the Royal Engineers mounted on . . . (other makes) and Triumphs in equal numbers'.

'They told me', he said, 'that the former had all crocked up, while the Triumphs were standing up to the severely unfair work in capital fashion'. Far from being locked up as aliens, the firm's German founders carried on supervising the supply of some 30,000 similar machines, all ironically for the exclusive use of the Allies.

Many of those two-speed, belt-driven military models were also fitted with the company's Gloria brand sidecars, whose separate, but wholly owned, premises would later overtake the motorcycle business and produce four-wheelers including one particularly famous Triumph motor-car carrying the Gloria model name.

The year 1914 and two British soldiers exchange despatches somewhere on the Italian front. The bike sideways to the camera is one of Triumph's trusty 4 hp military jobs

Above
Wonder what the rider on the left is puzzling about as this brace of Triumph veterans prepare to set off in the Sunbeam Motor Cycle Club's Annual Epsom to Brighton Pioneer Run

Below
No idea who he is, although I certainly admired this rider's style as he pobbled happily through this ford without a care in the world. His bike must surely have been fitted with a Bosch magneto!

Triumph and tragedy

Ricardo obliged with a four-cylinder engine for the company's first own-make car and a very advanced four-valve, single-cylinder motorcycle engine, immortalized ever since as Triumph's 'Riccy'.

Triumph's mass-produced 1925 model P came next to coincide with the entire world's economy taking a downturn. Rather than being an expensive-to-produce four-valver, it was little more than a cut-price version of the old H or SD, although at least the fans did get a replica of Victor Horsman's famous Brooklands track racer for the following year.

Production rose steadily to around 30,000 units per annum by 1929, which might sound a lot, but in real terms Triumph were still motorcycle industry minnows. Furthermore, they were relying increasingly on car manufacture to provide any real profits, which just could not be allowed to continue.

The pedal cycle and German TWN offshoots were sold off when Wall Street's prices fell through the floor, but even those measures proved too little too late, and all motorcycle production was abandoned as 1935 came to a close. (Although not before Val Page joined the company and introduced a new range of singles and also the company's first ever (650 cc) vertical twin.)

The year 1936 saw the sale, for a mere £5000, of what was left of the company's by then much troubled two-wheeler operation. It was bought, complete with Val Page's new designs, by Jack Sangster of Ariel, whose own single-cylinder motorcycle range, incidentally, was also Page designed.

Edward Turner, who had been Page's replacement at Ariel, was invited to switch factories and become the newly reconstituted Triumph Engineering Company's first general manager/chief designer, with a (suspected) low budget and a brief to give the products from these two separate companies decidedly less similar identities.

Turner rapidly introduced some very real improvements to his predecessor's Triumph designs, including fully enclosing their overhead valve gear. His claim of better new frames, however, is somewhat less supportable, for this latter exercise amounted to little more than his re-arranging the furniture.

One genuinely new item of typical Turner brilliance was his four-speed, constant-mesh and positive-stop-type foot-change gearbox.

His resulting late 1930s models, meanwhile, not only had to be rushed into production, but unusually were also released to the unsuspecting public during mid season and so they went without the benefit of any real publicity as would have been the case had they been given a proper 'Show' launch.

Next, Turner offered a supporting range of more highly-tuned 250, 350 and 500 cc super sports options, known respectively as the Tiger 70, 80 and 90.

Those soon much beloved models began a particularly long-running tradition, for the very name Tiger came to mean the top-of-range tuned

Left
Chris Ronald's superb 1922 SD (spring drive) model, which took several years to restore from a rusting hulk—quite an achievement

Above
The 4 hp engine department of Chris' SD. Note also the period-type detachable oil can, which is clipped just behind the main frame's rear down tube

Above

One of 1927's TT machines, complete with soldered fuel and oil tanks, although one engine exhaust port has been blanked off during the intervening years

models, and this applied right through until the Bonneville's arrival in 1959.

Val Page's original 650 cc parallel twin, which had twice won for Triumph the prestigious Maude's Trophy for 'outstanding reliability', meanwhile slipped quietly out of the range. As a replacement, Turner was working on a very special twin-cylinder design of his own, which at first also looked as though it would be unveiled as a Tiger.'

Triumph's catalogue for 1938, and all of the advertising for the new 500 cc parallel twin certainly showed it painted in the Tiger's sportier colours, rather than the eventual Speed Twin's Amaranth red, although it was already being referred to as the latter.

Maybe it had been intended as the Tiger 100 from the outset, who knows. Then perhaps Turner recalled his earlier marketing exercise of finding a fresh market for the cooking singles re-tuned as Tigers and thought he could milk the cow again, for certainly the tuned Tiger 100 version did arrive just like them, his usual year later!

Whichever, the new twin-cylinder engine also slotted straight into the existing range's rolling chassis.

Perhaps Turner hadn't yet learned how to be the supreme product (and self) publicist that he undoubtedly became later, for as far as the media were concerned the new twins arrived with more of a whimper than the definite roar of a Tiger. Little did they know that these were, and arguably would continue to be, the most significant products in British motorcycle history.

Above
Turner's immortal Speed Twin in its original combined Magdyno pre-war guise with a front-wheel-driven speedometer gearbox

'Experimental 1', the actual 1937 prototype Tiger 100 is owned now and still used by David Jenkin. Even the silver stripes on black-painted mudguards are correct, for the story goes that Edward Turner stepped back to admire his handiwork, but did not like the colour scheme, so he reversed it to a black stripe on silver

Right
'Experimental 1's' engine deserves particularly close scrutiny. For instance, note the crankcase casting's almost pointed side profile, also the angular rather than softly blended cush-drive spring covering boss on the primary chain cases, all to be smoothed out for production

Left

Same water-splash as in the previous chapter, this time with a well used Speed Twin crossing it

Below

Triumphs carried their instruments on the petrol tank top until well after the war, with the furthest forward being an illuminating lamp

Blitzkrieg

Gathering war clouds in Europe found the still relatively young Triumph Engineering Group in an exceedingly healthy position, for the unprecedented sales success of Turner's new twins boosted their profitability during the late 1930s. Then general engineering work directed towards the greater war effort really filled the coffers.

All production still stemmed from Bettmann and Schulte's various original Coventry city-centre premises, which had merely been leased to Sangster when the car company sold its two-wheeler business. Edward Turner, meanwhile, was busily redesigning the rest of Triumph's range, putting almost the last vestiges of Val Page's versions behind him.

One of Turner's designs was the proposed 350 cc, overhead-valve model 3T twin, which owed very little in terms of engine component interchangeability to its immediate predecessor, the 500 cc 5T. Thus, it could be regarded as being somewhat of an extravagant gesture according to the British motorcycle industry's standard of the day.

Actual production of the 3T, however, had to be postponed until 1946 (simply because of the actions of a certain Herr Hitler), although when it did arrive it was never a sales success, nor was it worth waiting for, at least in my view (yes, I once owned one). On the other hand, Turner's arguably far more advanced 3TW side-valve twin really should have been a winner.

Even the ancestry of Triumph's much later 1980s machines can be traced directly back to this latter 1939 model, for just like them, it used a fully unit-construction engine and gearbox assembly. Similarly, it featured truly modern-style electrics, employing an alternator which was mounted on the end of the crankshaft.

Triumph had orders for tens of thousands of those military 3TW twins and 3HW (Tiger 80-based singles), as indeed did BSA, Norton and Matchless for their rival and, by comparison, outdated products. Sadly, that man Hitler and his Luftwaffe had other ideas.

The 3TW, and almost Triumph themselves, was killed off on 14 November 1940, a date that will forever live in infamy for the proud people of Coventry. That night Hitler's air force not only bombed their beloved cathedral, but also razed the entire city centre, including Triumph's factory.

Right
A Tiger 90 of 1938 and rare in the extreme. This one recently passed me at over 90 mph, so sorry officer, but I just had to chase after and photograph it, didn't I?

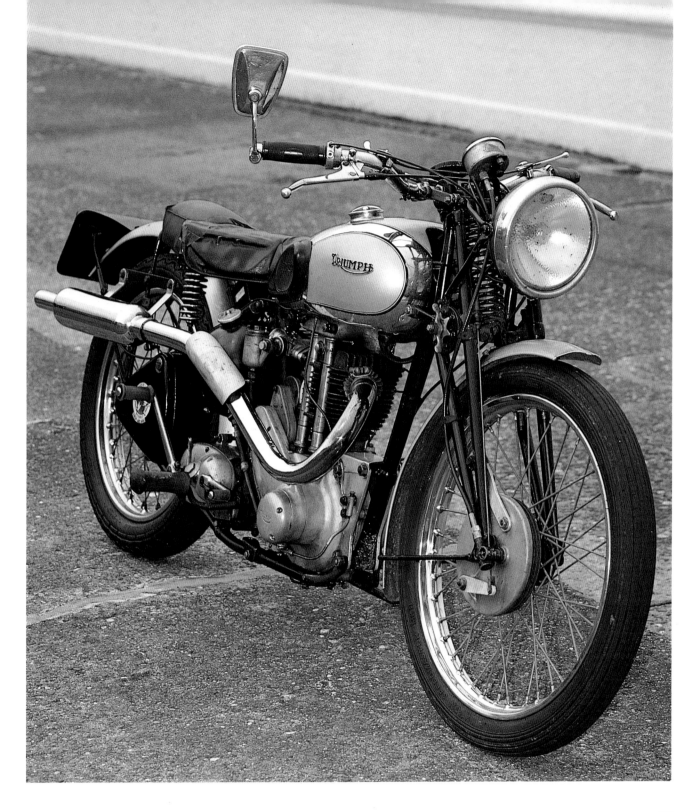

Above
A Tiger 100 of 1940, complete with the optional racing-type bronze cylinder head, also side check springs on each side of the front forks. With racing in mind, the megaphone silencers have quickly-detachable baffles

Right
T'other side of the same ultra-rare 1940 Tiger 100. Indeed, one wonders if this machine might possibly be the only survivor

THE "SPEED TWIN"

O. H. V. DOUBLE HIGH CAMSHAFT
VERTICAL TWIN. 63 mm. BORE BY
80 mm. STROKE. 498 C.C.

TRIUMPH PAT. Nos. 474963, 475860, 469635

Approximate Petrol Consumption:
100 m.p.g. at 40 m.p.h.

PRICE   Fully Equipped   **£80**

THE DE LUXE 3 H

O.H.V. SINGLE. 70 mm. BORE BY 89 mm.
STROKE. 343 C.C.

Approximate Petrol Consumption:
110 m.p.g. at 40 m.p.h.

PRICE   Fully Equipped   **£59**

THE DE LUXE 2 H

O.H.V. SINGLE. 63 mm. BORE BY 80 mm.
STROKE. 249 C.C.

Approximate Petrol Consumption:
120 m.p.g. at 40 m.p.h.

PRICE   Fully Equipped   **£54**

Left

The similarly ill-fated 'cooking' single and twin range for 1940. Note that year's Speed Twin also received fork side check springs, which were deleted again after the war

Above

The original 1940 caption to this picture states 'Mr. A. Jeffreys a well known civilian motor cyclist demonstrating rough riding to a hundred officers and men of the British Army's Northern Command'. Though the name was incorrectly spelt, it was actually THE Allan Jefferies, Triumph's oh so famous Manx Grand Prix road racer and trials star, riding one of their then new military ohv 350s

Right

All together girls, this is how to do it, at least according to their despatch rider instructor. Was it coincidental that these members of the Women's Royal Army Corps were issued with less sporting side-valvers, or deliberate?

The manufacturing patterns for this 3TW military twin were bombed out of existence during 1940, but it is worth comparing the unit-construction design with Turner's late 1950s and 1960s unit engines

Left
*Many of these military ohv 350s later
finished up as civilian trials bikes, for
being Tiger 80 based, they were
decidedly sporty*

*Jack Lilley won countless individual
trials and numerous overall
championships throughout the late 1940s
and early 1950s on his ex-WD job. He
also built a successful business out of
converting them for others*

PLEASE DO NOT TOUCH

1942 TRIUM

This generator set is on...
Triumph during the last wa...
for the RAF and used for s...
and supplying current for c...
manufacture. 24V 6KW DC...
cylinder fan cooled engine i...
governed to run at 5000rp...
started by handle, although...
The head and barrel are alloy...
on the Tiger 100 that won...
subsequently became the pro...
TR5 'Trophy' also used this...
shape being necessary to enal...
be fitted closely to the engm...
trailer mounted on motorcycl...
carry the generator to wherev...
During the war Triumph also mad...
tank track links, steering hou...
as well as 49,700 metric p...

Above

*Meriden's most famous wartime product
has to be their portable generator engine,
as used by the RAF. It lived on to power
the post-war Grand Prix racer and
Triumph's trials Trophy*

Out of the ashes

So total was the Blitz's devastation that, at first, there seemed no real hope of Triumph ever resuming production. Most of the engineering drawings, castings, patterns, spares, completed bikes and even the vital machine tools that made them had been destroyed overnight.

Incredibly, not one Triumph worker's life was lost in the bombing, and none was even seriously injured, despite the night shift having been caught working full tilt at the time. Such was both their and the management's morale that neither intended being put out of business.

Triumph's top brass spent months combing the Midlands area, looking for temporary alternative premises, whereas the workforce commenced searching Priory Street's ruins for anything, no matter how minor, that might have survived in the rubble. Very little was actually saved, but production recommenced during June 1941 in a tiny corrugated-iron chapel near Warwick, some 40 miles away. This was immediately, and irreverently, rechristened the 'Tin Tabernacle' by the workforce. It was hardly adequate, but would be Triumph's home for the foreseeable future.

Sadly, there could never by any hope of resuscitating Edward Turner's very advanced-specification 3TW model. Despite a vast order from the military,

Opposite page
A 1945 for 1946 production 3T (350), which should have arrived for 1940–1 had war not intervened. Having once owned one, I doubt if it was worth the long wait

Left
Also for 1946, the tuned 3T Tiger 85 version which, despite being catalogued, never did reach the market

every single drawing, pattern and component relating to this bike had been destroyed, and there was no time to start again.

However, Triumph still managed to build over 40,000 of their wartime 3HW single-cylinder military models, an amazing feat, bearing in mind that most were cast, machined and assembled in the old 'Tin Tabernacle'. They also produced some rather famous portable electrical generators.

The latter's role was to generate sufficient electricity to recharge the batteries in aircraft, such as the RAF's Lancaster bomber, wherever they stood on the airfield. From those dispersal points the same aircraft set out regularly to deliver both their and Triumph's own form of divine retribution!

Vital cooling for those basically standard twin-cylinder motorcycle engines was provided by a crankshaft-driven fan which blew air around the cylinders via ducting. To improve cooling efficiency, while also keeping weight down, the engines' top ends were cast in aluminium.

Meanwhile, Edward Turner left Triumph to join BSA during 1941, although he was to return four years later. Work had already commenced that year on building the new purpose-designed Meriden factory, right at the geographical centre of England and much nearer to the company's real home of Coventry.

Triumph probably never would have moved from their old rented and outdated Victorian premises had it not been for the bombings, yet with the resulting better premises and Churchillian Edward Turner's return to the fold in plenty of time to revamp their motorcycles for peacetime, one could say those same war clouds also had silver linings.

Only Triumph, among Britain's otherwise outdated and under-capitalized post-war motorcycle industry, would ever enjoy quite such modern facilities. Similarly, only Triumph would stand to benefit (as did the bombed-out German and Japanese industries) from a rare chance to make a fresh start, although as later history records, it would not be plain sailing.

Above
A Tiger 100 of 1948, having received a similar revamp to the Speed Twin, and shown here in greater detail

Right
Turner's comprehensively redesigned Speed Twin for 1946 gained telescopic front forks, and a separate magneto and dynamo, the last being moved to the front of its engine

Above
Take a close look at this Tiger 100's gear lever, for 1948 was the only year that Triumph used a bare metal and flat 'spoon-ended' pedal

Below
*Triumph's 1949 catalogue and an alpine
scene, hinting that two-wheeled life
around war-torn Europe was getting
under way again*

Racing Grand Prix

Of the many rows between Turner, the egotist, and his senior management colleagues, the unholiest concerned a certain one-off road racer devised and built by Freddie Clarke while his boss was away. In this instance, not even the fact that the bike won the 1946 Senior Manx Grand Prix was going to restore equanimity.

Clarke had been a pre-war Brooklands racer of no mean repute before becoming the head of Triumph's experimental department, so not only did he have racing in his blood, but hardly surprisingly he believed that it furthered the breed. The autocratic Turner, on the other hand, held the anti-racing view just as firmly. Perhaps more to the point, he was Clarke's and the company's boss.

Had Clarke and his personnel not been seen in such high profile at the races themselves, they might have got away with it, for his department would certainly have been entitled to build and test (although not officially race) any machine they developed. Turner, however was furious, despite the win, and not least because it all happened while he was away on one of his periodic long visits to America.

The machine which caused so much consternation was really little more than a stock Tiger 100 shorn of all unnecessary road impedimenta, and then lightened further by Clarke who fitted a wartime generator engine's alloy top half in place of the roadster's cast-iron components. He also fitted one of Turner's own prototype sprung hubs to give the bike a modicum of rear suspension.

All-up weight amounted to a mere 310 lb, and with some 40 bhp on tap, this bike developed almost five horses more than the same period's production Manx Nortons at a superior power-to-weight ratio. However, the post-war 'single-lungers' were well down on their pre-war power output due to the enforced de-tuning to cope with the prevailing lower octane (pool) petrol.

Norton rider Ken Bills had won the last pre-war race before hostilities intervened at a then record average speed of 84.81 mph, whilst also putting up a fastest ever single lap of 86.31 mph, so this same rider/bike combination would start as favourites in 1946 when these races resumed. That lone works special Triumph, being ridden by Ernie Lyons, rated hardly a mention.

Lyons had made his own Manx racing début in 1938 (when that man Bills also won), although he failed to get on the leader-board on that occasion before

Not Ernie Lyons riding to his famous Manx Grand Prix victory, but New Zealand's Sid Jensen two years later, winning the Visitor's Cup in the pukka international TT races

Right
*Rod Coates and Daytona 1984, the venue
where he won 1949's 100-mile amateur
race with this same Grand Prix, which he
has owned from new*

crashing on the fourth lap without ever really finding his way around this famous, but oh so difficult to memorize, $37\frac{3}{4}$-mile-long circuit. After a lapse of eight years, he would be starting as a veritable novice.

Race day dawned to absolutely appalling conditions with almost impenetrable mist on the mountain and torrential rain falling virtually everywhere else. Indeed, it was so bad that there was some doubt that the races could even be held, yet Lyons recalls being delighted with the weather because he knew it would even things up by greatly lowering race speeds.

Norton won in 1947, but E. G. Crossley used just such an over-the-counter bike to lead all the way and, hence, repeat Lyons' victory during 1948's race. Similarly, Rod Coates stamped his superiority on Daytona's annual amateur 100-mile American beach race. Beyond those few successes, however, the Grand Prix proved both fragile and, at times, spectacularly unreliable.

Below
David Lynch's ex-Arthur Wheeler racing Grand Prix model dates back to 1950, and once led a hectic life in racing's Continental circus

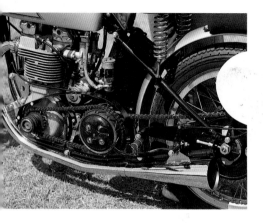

Above

GP drive-side, showing the remote float chamber set-up above Triumph's original, yet surprisingly crude, primary chain guard

Perhaps Turner was right and Triumph should have stayed out of racing, for although these collectors' bikes now fetch vast sums of money, they were once looked upon with considerable embarrassment in true racing circles. Incidentally, it's doubtful if more than 200 were made, with most of them going to America.

Subsequent history reveals that rather more of these production racers (and Trophies) have survived than Triumph ever made, which just goes to show that the factory were not alone in grafting square cylinder barrels on to ordinary Tiger 100s (although they didn't need to re-stamp the engine numbers). So nowadays, it really has become an instance of 'Let the buyer beware'!

'Not knowing the mountain section well', he recalled, 'I just followed the yellow line painted down the middle of the road', whereas everyone else floundered about, peering through the mist, looking for their braking or peel-off points. Lyons, the canny Irish farmer, sure enough led them home every inch of the way.

The rather slow 76.74 mph victory was not without incident, however, for he suffered a heart-stopping, monumental slide on the last lap which, at the time, he put down to a momentary loss of concentration caused when the bike's rev-counter suddenly failed. Much nearer the truth, however, was that the Triumph's main frame chose that moment to snap clean in two where it met the engine's front mounting plates.

Not unnaturally, Triumph hushed up that fact for many a long year, although a post-race check on the rev-counter's loss of function did indeed reveal a broken cable which the company admitted. They did not stay that it had snapped as a result of the severed frame flexing. Not that it mattered much, for in the meantime Edward Turner had returned from America!

Almost immediately, he threw a highly publicized celebratory dinner in Lyons' honour, despite carpeting everyone else involved at the factory. This caused Freddie Clarke and Bert Hopwood, who was Turner's number two, to resign and join the rival AMC Group. It all happened, unfortunately, amidst accusations of E.T. having a hopelessly egotistical and objectionable attitude.

Sadly, Clarke died soon after in a road accident, whereas Hopwood would not return to Triumph for another 14 years. One particular touch of irony was that Turner himself eventually unveiled a production replica racer, named, of course, Grand Prix after the famous victory of Clarke's brainchild.

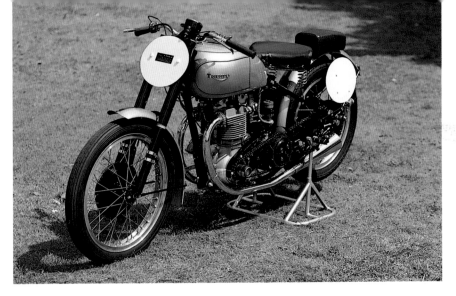

Left
Well worth a second look at Dave Lynch's newly-restored Grand Prix

Below
Robin Sherry on his stripped-for-action roadster Tiger 100 during a 1940s Clubmans TT. Triumph were about to offer a bolt-on race kit for this model which, in turn, spelled the end of the Grand Prix

Generator Trophies

Freddie Clarke's successful Grand Prix formula of mixing components was repeated during 1948, but this time by Henry Vale, who was Triumph's off-road competition supremo. He built three very special works International Six Day Trial machines, using the 5T roadster's milder-mannered bottom end rather than the tuned Tiger 100's.

The simple reasoning behind this second experiment was that Triumph hadn't otherwise got anything suitable to enter in the first post-war International which was about to be held at San Remo in Italy. Towards winning this event, even the British government were offering some highly unusual extra support.

You see, all of the raw materials necessary for building motorcycles were still rationed at that time by Britain's early post-war Ministry of Supply unless, that is, the finished products were quite definitely destined for export or, as in

Below

A picture taken some years ago of my own, then freshly-restored, very early Trophy (registered JRU 823). Wonder where it is now?

Above
*Allan Willmot has owned this 1949
version from new, and it is still totally
original, as seen here except for the
Dunlop rubber saddle, road tyres, and
missing pillion pad*

the ISDT's instance, had a good chance of becoming a export-order-winning shop window. With the recent Axis powers having been banned from competing, the Ministry had seen a chance for British products to cash in.

Each of our major motorcycle manufacturers was informed officially that they would receive unlimited supplies of materials for the purpose of competing in Italy. Furthermore, there was the implication that should they do well and those much-needed export orders actually materialized, then the materials would keep coming, which meant increased output and turnover.

Triumph, however, hadn't a competition bike in their existing range, yet they knew that they HAD to enter, despite not having the time or materials left to design and build anything totally new. It was from this *Catch-22* situation that Henry Vale's three specials came to their rescue.

Vale lashed up his comp. jobs from standard Speed Twin roadsters fitted with trials tyres and running on lowered overall gearing. He grafted on the

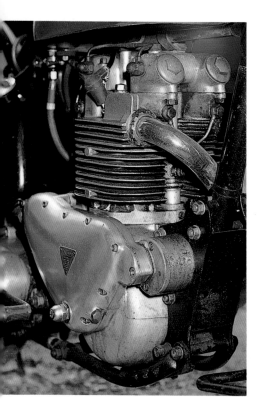

Above

Note the two cast bosses on Allan Willmot's bike's cylinder barrel. These would have been drilled and tapped to accept an air cooling cowling if for military generator use, but not of course on a GENUINE Grand Prix or Trophy

alloy generator engine top ends, just as Clarke before him, and sent Jim Alves, Bert Gaymer and Allan Jefferies off to Italy on a wing and a prayer to ride them.

These 'bitsa' machines were not called Trophy yet, although they were about to earn this very famous title. Messrs Alves, Gaymer and Jefferies did a superhuman job in not only surviving the event's full six days without loss of marks, but also won three individual gold medals whilst bringing home the even more prestigious Manufacturer's Team Trophy.

This was quite a phenomenal and almost mind-boggling off-road achievement that can be likened to entering and winning today on three equally unsuited modern long-wheelbase roadsters. However, that talented trio later admitted in private that they didn't really know how they had managed it, for their bikes actually handled like camels!

Not surprisingly, Triumph unveiled the over-the-counter replicas soon after, and even less surprisingly called them Trophys. However, these were, and are, the only instance in motorcycling history that I can recall where the resulting supposed copies far surpassed the originals in every aspect.

The November 1948-onwards production machines received an all-new, far better, and very much shorter-wheelbase chassis, for instance, which also formed the basis of the later TRW military twin. Overall weight fell even further to a mere 295 lb dry, despite a full lighting kit being fitted, which made the Trophy by far the lightest of all such competition 500s.

Messrs Jefferies, Alves and Gaymer used Trophys themselves for the 1949, 1950 and 1951 Internationals, winning individual gold medals and the Manufacturer's award on each occasion (the only make and riders to do so). There would also be many more medals won by privately-entered Trophys in various amateur riders' hands.

The 1951-onwards machines worked just as well, but were fitted with the Tiger 100's newer fine-pitch, round-fin cylinders and cylinder heads because supplies of the wartime generator engine's square, parallel-ported top half had been finally exhausted by then. As a result, the Trophy lost much of what had been its previous square-barrel aura.

Left

A made-up bike, or perhaps one which has merely lost its original cylinder barrel? Who knows, but as the bosses are drilled, this one certainly saw military service

Below

W. H. Davies on Treworgie Hill during 1958's semi-sporting Lands End Trial. His bike is a 1952 version with the later fine-pitch-finned engine. It is virtually devoid of bright plating because that was the year of the world chrome shortage

Chrome-plate was back for 1953, together with a new duck-egg blue instead of silver paint scheme. The fine-fin upper engine castings, featured here on David Jenkin's bike, were also several pounds lighter than their square predecessors

Above
The year 1951 and the cover of Triumph's annual catalogue featuring one of Oxley's famous cartoons, showing the new Thunderbird meeting the old 500 cc Speed Twin

Thunderbirds are go

Early in 1949 Edward Turner instructed his works development department to build up a rather interesting Speed Twin engine. This had shorter connecting rods running on a one-off special crankshaft that featured an extra 2 mm throw, and pistons running in a standard cylinder barrel overbored from the normal 63 mm to 71 mm.

None of this engine's castings needed changing, as the Speed Twin's cylinders had plenty of surplus 'meat'. So by merely altering the bore and stroke from 63×80 mm to 71×82 mm, Turner came up with a cheap-to-produce 649 cc engine capable of being dropped straight into the existing 498 cc machine's chassis. This hybrid 650 produced a massive extra $7\frac{1}{2}$ bhp over the 500 by the time proving trials commenced around the highways and byways near Coventry. Thus, it caused more than a few local and suddenly disgruntled Tiger 100 owners, who had been passed by it, to visit the factory and complain that there must be something very wrong as they had just been blown off by a 'cooking' Speed Twin!

All was eventually revealed, however, in a blaze of Ivor Davies-inspired publicity on 16 September 1949 when four pre-production 650s were officially named as Triumph's new Thunderbirds. They were despatched under their own steam from Meriden on what was to be a high-speed junket to France.

Davies' plan was that three of the four bikes should attempt covering 500 miles at a 90 mph average around Montlhéry's famous banked race circuit just outside Paris, then finish the proceedings with flying laps at over 100 mph. This was some challenge in those days on the prevailing low-octane ($72°$) petrols, yet the Thunderbirds all made it quite easily.

Turner himself had devised the model name and drawn the famous petrol tank motif with, as always, the American market primarily in mind. Those swooping birds play an important role in North American Indian mythology, and it was towards that great continent's straighter roads that this entire exercise was aimed.

Shattering performance, quality, reliability and stamina rapidly became the key words when the era's road testers were describing this brilliant new 650 that outwardly was the same size as a 500, yet it could also be incredibly docile, which is precisely why it became such a great favourite amongst sidecar riders as well.

A tuned Tiger 110 version came along later, although at the cost of losing some of the base model's unfussed tractability and more pleasant manners. Neither version handled brilliantly, especially in solo form and pushed anywhere near to the limit, but as long-distance touring hauliers, however, these bikes were unequalled.

Above
London's Metropolitan Police tried two-way radios on motorcycles first during February 1951. They soon found that they needed more electrical power than Joe Lucas' dynamos were providing, resulting in the later 5TAs and 6Ts gaining crankshaft-mounted, high-output alternators

TRIUMPH
Patent Nos.
475860, 474963
482024

Thunderbird

With its tremendous reserve of power, the 650c.c. "Thunderbird" is the choice of the man who really needs performance. It is at its best when road conditions permit prolonged fast cruising or there is a heavy sidecar to be hauled. Low petrol consumption is a feature of the "Thunderbird".

SPECIFICATION

WHEELS. Triumph design, with heavy duty dull-plated spokes. Dunlop tyres.
ELECTRICAL EQUIPMENT. Famous Triumph pioneered A.C. lighting-ignition set eliminating separate dynamo and magneto. Wide angle rear/stop light. Powerful Lucas 7" built in headlamp with combined reflector/front lens assembly, "pre-focus" bulb and adjustable rim. Separate parking light.

TOOLBOX. All steel, large capacity, with quick-release fastener. Complete set of good quality tools and grease gun.
MUDGUARDS. Efficient "D" shaped guards with central rib. Rear guard detachable for rear wheel accessibility.
NACELLE. Neat streamline shell integral with top of forks, encloses headlamp,

instruments and switchgear. All instruments rubber mounted and internally illuminated.
SPEEDOMETER. Smiths 120 m.p.h. (or 180 km.p.h.) chronometric type with r.p.m. scale internal illumination and trip recorder.
OTHER DETAILS. Well sprung saddle; quick-action adjustable twist grip; integral horn push; comfortable adjustable handlebars; rubber knee grips; tank parcel grid.

For Technical Details see Back Cover.

Headlamp Nacelle.
Patent No. 645670.

Above

Coil ignition as well as alternator electrics for 1954, and therefore a forerunner of the later police Saint model

Left

A recently spotted early Thunderbird, not quite the right colour, but obviously still giving good service

Far left

ROSPA's 1962 Motorcycle of the Year competition and the late Harry Louis, under whom I served on the 'Blue-un', is making very sure that this later-specification, sprung-hub 6T's rider can stop his outfit on a sixpence

Trouble in store

There was nothing remotely feline or graceful about most 1940s and early 1950s motorcycles, not least because virtually all manufacturers continued using complex, and usually ultra-heavy, pre-war-type main frames. The various post-war bits were hung on almost as afterthoughts.

Motorcycles in general started life this way, from the days when an engine was slung beneath a pedal cycle's crossbar, and no one, other than Philip Vincent (of Vincent Motor Cycles), ever really stepped back to query the overall visual concept. At least, that is, until December 1950 when Edward Turner's new designs almost caused a calamity. The occasion was the unveiling of his superbly-styled 1951 range at the London show, where so many excited visitors pushed and shoved to get a closer look at them that the entire stand literally collapsed. Fortunately, no one was seriously injured.

Most visually exciting was the new Tiger 100 with its fine-fin-pitch, die-cast aluminium cylinder head and barrel. However, all had received beautifully re-styled and painted (instead of chrome-plated) fuel tanks, along with swish badges and a top-mounted luggage rack where instruments had previously been. A truly superb looking headlamp nacelle faired in much of each machine's front end whilst hiding the normally messy control and electrical cables.

Turner's new sprung rear hub and Triumph's first ever dualseat also came as standard on the Tiger 100. Mere words alone fail to express just how well these models were received, for Turner alone had managed to bridge the visual fashion gap between yesteryear's rigid machines and the coming springers.

Behind the scenes, things were not nearly so healthy, however, for Meriden were taking on the entire industry with but four fairly similar 500 cc and over machines. The rival BSA organization, on the other hand, boasted 19, encompassing a far wider range of engine capacities, so they were biting deeply into the prime export markets.

BSA's highly profitable Bantam commuter model also sold by the hundreds of thousands, funding things like new pivoted-rear-fork frames for their immortal Gold Stars, yet Triumph had neither sufficient factory space, nor any smaller-capacity models with which to fight back.

A protracted series of discussions between Jack Sangster and BSA's management followed during 1951, resulting in Meriden being sold to its Small Heath rivals for £2½ million later that year. Supposedly, this was to safeguard Triumph's long-term future, although as we all now know, fate eventually decreed otherwise.

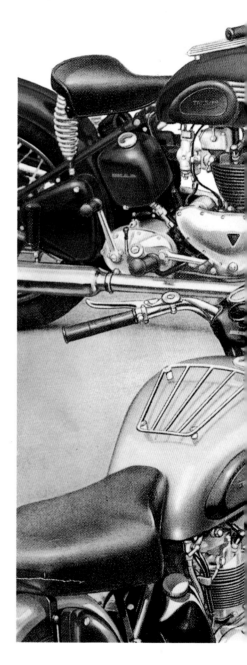

★ **PERFORMANCE**

STAMINA

★ **QUALITY**

1 FRONT BRAKE. Exceptionally powerful with new cast iron drum.
2 FRONT NUMBER PLATE. Unique Triumph design; no sharp edges.
3 TELESCOPIC FRONT FORK. For comfort and first class steering.
4 NACELLE. Streamlines lamp and instruments into easy-clean shell.
5 FRAME. Rigid cradle type for good handling at high and low speeds.
6 TIMING COVER. Highly polished, easy to clean, smart appearance.

10 PARCEL GRID. Unique Triumph feature. Ideal for light baggage.
11 TRIUMPH TWIN-SEAT. For solo and pillion riding. Luxurious latex foam.
12 TOOL BOX. Ample room for standard tool kit and extra items.
13 REAR MUDGUARD. Detaches in one piece from behind the saddle.

TRIUMPH FEATURES FOR BETTER RIDING

7 GEARBOX Designed for fast changing with a particularly sweet and light clutch.
8 AIR CLEANER. The answer to dust; neat and unobtrusive.
9 PETROL TANK. A smooth easily-cleaned tank of large capacity.

14 SPRING WHEEL. Comfortable ride at all speeds. Powerful 8" brake.
15 SILENCERS. Reduce exhaust note with minimum of back pressure.
16 REAR NUMBER PLATE. Triumph design with lifting handle combined.

Right
*Modern-style coil ignition, yet still a
rigid frame, even for 1954's Speed Twin*

Left

The year 1954 again and the front end of a shell blue Tiger 110, surely the prettiest roadster Triumph ever made

Right

Nice as Turner's headlamp nacelle looked, it wasn't actually very practical, for by enclosing the handlebar centres, it prevented them from ever being changed to different shape bends. The light-gauge tinplate nacelle assembly also distorted easily and was exceedingly vulnerable to any knocks

Lightweights in a class of their own

It is sad to reflect, but there were 38 other British motorcycle manufacturers exhibiting fulsome ranges at London's Earls Court in November 1952, when Triumph's new diminutive 149 cc Terrier was popularly voted star of the show. Now all, except Norton, are merely names from the distant past.

Then, however, the picture looked rosy indeed, for their order books were full, raw materials shortages were easing, and previous low fuel octanes were improving. This allowed most to offer ever more super-tuned models aimed at the great American market.

Below

John Stephenson's magnificently restored plunger-framed 149 cc Terrier, one of the very few lightweights I have ever lusted after

Left
*Even from above, the Terrier looks like a
big bike. Perhaps more importantly it
also performed like one*

Above
*The same machine's engine seen from the
opposite side and in greater detail*

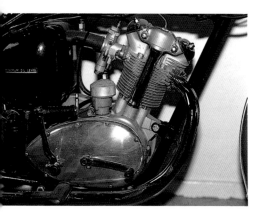

Above
An enlarged Terrier, or rather one of the very first 199 cc Cubs. This one also owned by John Stephenson, lucky man

Right
Swinging-arm suspension improved the Cub's ride, although I was never keen on the later styling or the smaller wheels

Only those manufacturers who relied on bought-in Villiers two-stroke engines had any problems, which they didn't know about until the show opened and they saw Triumph's brilliant new arrival. It certainly must have caused more than a few hurriedly-called board meetings.

Here, after all, was the first lightweight to look and go like a heavyweight. Furthermore, it enjoyed larger and better brakes, and was easier to start, service and ride than its rivals. It offered the quality associated with Triumph's famous name along with a unique four-stroke engine, whereas they were all stuck with a common and relatively agricultural powerplant.

It is doubtful that any other lightweight machine has ever made quite such an immediate, long-lasting and well deserved impact or gone down in motorcycling's long-term history as being so major a milestone. You could have taken the name badges off this bike before placing it on any of the show's other 42 stands (including BMW, Moto Guzzi and Lambretta) and the Terrier would still have been instantly recognizable as a Triumph.

As a personal aside, in those days I regularly cycled several miles each night just to be able to gaze longingly at the selfsame show bike, for it was exhibited for a while in my local Triumph dealers, Blacknells of Derby. However, I had about as much hope of buying one as jumping the moon.

I never did buy a Terrier, but subsequently I covered tens of thousands of cut-and-thrust miles on the larger 199 cc Cub versions, which came in a year later. I've also trialed, scrambled and grass-tracked them for most of the last 30 odd years, hence perhaps my over-glowing opinions.

'Mooneyes' John Cooper, with whom I happened to grow up, virtually made his road racing name on a Cub when incredibly he rode rings around the late, great, Bob McIntyre mounted on, of all things, his 500 cc Manx Norton. Furthermore, he did so at the latter's Scottish home circuit, and as *Motor Cycle News'* man, I was there to report it, too.

Roy Peplow's Cub similarly made trialing history during 1961 by becoming the first (and last) lightweight to win the ultra-tough Scottish Six Days, whereas since then Dave Thorpe has won the Pre-65 Classic Scottish One Day event on his little Triumph a record four times. Can't be bad for a mass-produced commuter-type machine which is now of very considerable vintage.

BSA finally stopped even the 90 mph Sports Cub's production because it threatened their own brand of lightweights. Then later in a quite ironic move they discontinued making those, too, on the ill-founded presumption that if they let the encroaching Japanese have the lightweight market they might not make anything bigger!

Formerly my own ex-1963 works team trials Cub, a lovely little bike which gave me hours of mainly trouble-free enjoyment in literally hundreds of trials

Above
The year 1955 saw in Amal's then new Monobloc carburettor, although beyond that there were few other changes

Right
An alloy-engined, swinging-arm-framed Tiger 100 of 1954, which always looked faster and sportier than the same period's T110 with its cast-iron top end. In fact, it lacked the grunt of the latter and was rather more rattly

Opposite page
David Hampson's 1954 Tiger 110 photographed in the Isle of Man during TT week 1990 and looking a million dollars

New frames for old

Not even Edward Turner could ignore the inevitable march towards full pivoted-fork rear suspension for ever, so at last he unveiled a new swinging-arm frame for the 1954 season. At first, however, it would only be fitted to the Tiger 100 and new 650 cc model Tiger 110, not the entire range.

The Cub and Terrier soldiered along with their plungers, and all other models continued as rigids. Quite incredibly in an era when all other makers already offered rear suspension as standard, Triumph still listed their limited-movement sprung hub as a decidedly expensive optional extra.

High-performance fans of the day were certainly impressed with the new and fully-sprung 110, however. Its Thunderbird-based engine benefited from

Previous page

The other side of the same 110 featured in the previous picture, and looking almost exactly like the bike I used to own

Above

One of the earliest competition Trophys to receive swinging-arm rear suspension, being ridden to good purpose here by Triumph enthusiast Dave Naylor. (The seat pad is not original)

Right

A Trophy as supplied for 1955. A dualseat is correct, but this one looks as though it might be home-made

having higher-compression pistons, hotter cams, and larger inlet valves and carburettor. Collectively, these gave an 8 bhp increase to 42 bhp, as opposed to the 'cooking' model's 34 bhp.

Each of the new swinging-arm Tigers also received a very much improved 8 in. front brake, which came ready fitted with racing-type air scoops, and even the rigid-framed Thunderbird showed a pointer to the future because it had been given a high-output, crankshaft-mounted alternator. This replaced the more normal dynamo in readiness to power the two-way radios of numerous police forces.

The only other new bike for 1954 was the TRW, which was intended for military use. It employed mainly rigid Trophy cycle parts to house its cut-price side-valve engine. With the exception of one still-born works prototype, this long-running model would never receive any form of rear suspension.

Fortunately, not even 1954's mis-matched frame situation lasted for very much longer (it couldn't have, as no one would have bought them). All but the lightweights and previously-mentioned TRW finally inherited the two Tiger twins' superior swinging-armed chassis for the 1955 season.

Changes for 1956 were largely limited to details like rubber-mounted fuel tanks, a pilot lamp that was integral with the headlight rather than being

underslung as before, adjustable steering stop bolts, and an improved centre
stand. Perhaps most importantly on the Tiger 110 was a new cast-aluminium
cylinder head instead of an iron one.

American Johnny Allen had just gone to the Bonneville salt flats in Utah
and ridden his Tiger 110-engined, torpedo-like projectile to a new two-way,
two-wheeled land speed record of 193 mph. Armed with one of these later
cylinder heads, further adapted to accept twin carburettors, he was about to
considerably top that.

Allen's second attempt raised his speed to just over 214 mph, but this time it
only counted as a new American rather than world record. Although there was
never any doubt whatsoever about the competence of the timekeepers,
unfortunately, they had not been affiliated to the Federation Internationale
Motorcycliste which was the official international ratifying body.

Triumph long advertised that they had captured this 214.4 mph record, adding in very small print that it was 'subject to official confirmation'. Sadly, this never came, due to the political rivalry between the FIM and the American AMA.

This sorry situation dragged on for another two years whilst the international lawyers earned rich pickings from the resulting litigation. Indeed, it was never satisfactorily resolved, so Triumph eventually cocked a snook by renaming what should have been the 1958 for 1959 twin-carburettor T110 as the Bonneville.

Above and overleaf
This, at the time, was my own 1959 Trophy, which should have been fitted with the horrible, later-type full-width front hub/brake assembly. However, to be honest, I threw it away, and although I retained the period fuel tank badges, they didn't exactly set me alight!

Above
Brian Relph's 1959 Thunderbird 6T in
that year's dark polychromatic grey—not
a restored bike, for at the time, it had only
covered 7074 miles from new

Left

The 1961 ivory and black, pre-unit Tiger 100 considerably overlapped Turner's unit-construction engine design, so it was the last of a long line and also very short-lived

Right

Beauty may lie in the eye of the beholder, but compare this full-width front hub 1961 Tiger 100 with 1954's, then ask yourself if Triumph's 1960s designs were going backwards or forwards

650 cc Trophy

Jim Alves rode a rather interesting 650 cc prototype, based on a Tiger 110 engine in a spare 500 cc trials Trophy chassis, to win his bronze medal in 1955's International Six Day Trial. However, neither it nor 1956's production version were intended as serious trialsters, for their real all-conquering forte was as US desert racers.

They were a little too heavy and rorty for European off-road tastes, and they didn't handle particularly well, even for scrambling. In the longer-distance stateside enduros, however, they literally won everything going, although the 650 Trophy's brightest of many bright moments somehow still managed to occur in Europe.

This happened when a professional Hollywood stunt man, named Bud Ekins, came over to double for star Steve McQueen in a war epic, *The Great*

Below

This TR6C Trophy of 1959 vintage might look like it has alloy cylinder barrels, but in fact they were cast-iron merely painted silver

Above

Slightly worn and frayed at the edges maybe, but why not, for this is Bud Ekins' actual 1962 ISDT gold medal-winning machine, preserved exactly as it finished in that event

Left

The powerplant of 1961's American-specification TR6R desert racer, so beloved Stateside, incidentally, which is where most Trophys went

Above
*Even in honourable retirement, Ekins'
650 still has all of its major components
paint or wire sealed, as carried out
originally by the Six Day Trial
scrutineers to stop any illicit substitution
of parts*

Escape. This was being filmed in Germany, where Ekins worked out that if he stayed on he could compete in the 1962 ISDT, which was about to commence in Bavaria.

Ekins ordered a new standard Trophy from Meriden and arranged for it to be brought out to him by Triumph's works riders, who would be arriving on the eve of the trial. Its final preparation was limited to his fitting a pair of the Americans' beloved ultra-high-rise 'cow horn' style handlebars, and even more unusually for off-road use, a rear view mirror.

No one expected miracles of him, for he would be using stock tackle against the might of the best equipped works teams, Triumph's included. Far from being overawed, however, Ekins literally stormed away to win the overall unlimited capacity class award and with it, of course, a gold medal. It really was an unparalleled achievement.

Left

Tank-top map case cum tool bag, American wide bars, and probably the only rear-view mirror ever to grace such a competition machine. It was on t'other side when Ekins raced it in Germany, however, not least because they and the Yanks ride on the 'wrong' side of the road!

Below

Apologies to owner Brian Moore, but this is a BSA-inspired TR6C Trophy of 1971, a real travesty bearing Small Heath's stamp all over it, and not a proud end

Birthdays and 'bathtubs'

Jack Sangster's Triumph Engineering Co. Ltd reached its 21st birthday during 1957, and celebrated by unveiling Edward Turner's totally new design, unit-construction, 350 cc engined Twenty One twin model. The immediate response by members of the buying public was either love at first sight, or loathing, with virtually nothing between.

Looking back now, as one of the original detractors, even I would have to admit that this bike was really remarkable. However, rather as happened years later to the Ford Motor Company and their Sierra, the Twenty One had been styled just a wee bit ahead of its time.

We knockers did not necessarily dislike or distrust the Twenty One's unit method of engine construction, although many quite rightly foresaw it as heralding the eventual passing of their beloved pre-unit powerplants. Rather the bike's wimpish rear-end enclosure and dainty, undersized wheels concerned us greatly.

Turner's Twenty One was really guilty of breaking with the era's more acceptable and traditional designs. Thus, it would be judged by an unready public as being effeminate, unsporting, and certainly not quite a man's bike. All this suggested that even the Maestro might have had to rethink his plans.

Far from dispensing with the hated rear enclosure, which was soon irreverently christened the 'bathtub', Turner overbored the 348 cc unit engine from 58.25 to 69 mm, which opened it out to 500 (498 cc). Then he marketed this second version with enclosed rear end, as the 1959-onwards replacement for the pre-unit Speed Twin.

Now it really was only a matter of time before all other Triumphs followed this particular unit-construction path, and no bad thing either because they soon became far superior engines. Meanwhile, the hated small wheels began to grow again, whilst the equally dubious 'bathtubs' steadily shrank and then quietly faded away.

Comparing machines from different design generations is difficult and inevitably subject to personal opinions. However, much as I respected the quality of the pre-unit jobs, nonetheless there are no doubts in my own mind that the later bikes offered a better overall package and were definitely superior to ride.

The 650s even retained the pre-unit version's bore and stroke and many of its components, so they hardly changed in terms of engine power or performance. The newer 500s, on the other hand, being overbored short-stroke 350 cc engines at heart, were different in feel, although not necessarily better or worse.

Previous page

Kay Ryan's smashing little 350 cc Twenty One of 1957 vintage—immaculate still, yet a hard working bike

Above

The other side of Kay's machine, showing the two rubber bungs in the rear 'bathtub', behind which go the touring pannier fittings

Left
*The larger 'bathtub' version from 1960,
bored out to near enough 500 cc and re-
christened the Speed Twin*

Below
*Same 1960 model 5TA Speed Twin, and
there would soon be a similarly unit-
construction Tiger 100 joining the fold*

Overleaf
*By 1963 the backlash-prone distributor
had been replaced by camshaft-driven
contact breakers housed within the
engine's outer timing covers, as illustrated
on this Tiger 90 model*

Above

The 1963 Thunderbird also received the 'bathtub' treatment, but as on the rest of that year's range, it was a much abbreviated version

Right

A naked behind again for 1966, the bike mind you, not Lillian Jacobs who is seen at the time riding a well-equipped Tiger 100

Bonneville's revenge

On the morning of 6 September 1962 a small group of figures could be seen busily working away on a lone cigar-shaped object standing amidst Utah's vast acres of salt flats. Then, just as dawn broke, the previous, almost uncanny, quietness was shattered by the sudden roar of a twin-cylinder engine being revved up to full power.

This was no accidental happening, but a serious attempt at revenge involving Bill Johnson, a 38-year-old lorry driver, and Joe Dudek, who was chief mechanic of North American Aviation. They were about to prove to the recalcitrant FIM, who wouldn't recognize the previous world record, just how fast a Triumph could really go.

Powering their device was a rear-mounted, unsupercharged, 649 cc Bonneville engine, which had been fitted with 11:1 pistons and was running

Below

The legend reads T110, but this is 1959's actual twin-carburettor prototype Bonneville, photographed before Triumph got around to making a replacement T120 engine timing cover identity plate

on alcohol fuel. Bill Johnson, its rider—or perhaps pilot in this instance—lay in an almost prostrate position in the nose of this 17 ft long shell.

Standard Triumph wheels and brakes were used, but fitted with specially designed Dunlop six-ply 3.50 × 19 in. racing tyres, their treads being trimmed down to a mere 1 mm to help reduce flexing and keep them cooler at the anticipated ultra-high speeds. Unusually, there was no parachute or additional means of braking.

They had made very sure that the timekeepers involved were all FIM approved rather than risk repeating Johnny Allen's earlier fate when his 214.4 mph record went unratified. As Johnson had already topped 230 mph (unofficially) during preparation, there was every hope of success for Dudek's missile.

The salt flats were not in nearly such good condition, however, on the morning of the official record attempt, reducing the cigar's maximum speed to 227.17 mph out and 222.03 mph back, to average 224.57 mph over the two-way measured flying kilometer. Even so, this was more than enough to smash the previous best of 211.04 mph, which had been held by NSU and Wilhelm Herz of Germany since 1956.

Indeed, these were exciting times generally for Triumph, as John Wright won America's prestigious 500-mile Jack Pine Enduro that same week on his little Tiger Cub. On the home front, Edward Turner had been spending most

Above

The year 1960 brought a new duplex frame along with this pearl grey and azure blue colour scheme. Turner's long-lived headlamp nacelle had finally given way to a separate, chrome-plated headlamp.

Bonneville salt flats, Utah, 5 September 1962, and Bill Johnson had just hoisted the motorcycle world speed record to 224.57 mph in Joe Dudek's 'flying cigar', laying the ghost of Triumph's and Johnny Allen's earlier disappointment

of his time at BSA, so Bert Hopwood at last returned from Norton.

Hopwood lost very little time in persuading Doug Hele, who was Norton's brilliant development engineer, to cross the fence and join him. Then, with this duo at the helm, things really began to happen, including a near total redesign of the Bonneville. This went to a unit-construction engine for 1963.

This was the version about which the late, and much lamented, motorcycle journalist Bob Currie coined his famous phrase, 'it looks like it is doing 100 mph even when it's standing still'. It really was a 'Jekyll and Hyde'-like fire breather, although despite new and much improved front forks, its handling still remained slightly suspect.

An extra 1 in. of fork travel, achieved by fitting longer stanchions, made a definite improvement for 1965, but the real handling breakthrough came a year later when Hele changed the steering head angle from 65 to 62 degrees. This finally did the trick, for henceforth the Bonneville would steer as well as anything else around.

From then onwards, it became a detail honing operation, including the addition of a better twin-leading-shoe front brake, Amal's much improved Concentric carburettors, and Lucas' individually adjustable 6 CA contact breaker assembly, which arrived collectively for 1968. Thus, the best 'Bonnie' was very nearly there.

The year 1969 brought twin electric horns and a different front brake cable tie-up arrangement, which greatly increased even the new brakes' efficiency. The engine's method of breathing was changed in the light of racing experience to 'un-timed' for 1970 when this model became the last true all-Triumph 650 cc Bonneville, and certainly the best.

By then the BSA parent group had unfortunately got themselves into deep financial trouble and were increasingly skimming off Meriden's still considerable profits in an attempt to bale themselves out. As if that wasn't bad enough, they were about to foist Meriden with a new Group standard chassis.

Triumph then lost literally months of production through altering their engines to make them fit into those Umberslade Hall committee-designed, oil-carrying frames that really never worked. To say that the results were 'bastards' would be the understatement of the year!

Never before in the history of motorcycle design had two such major manufacturers come out with anything as bad as those 1971 models. Indeed, quite apart from the truly awful visual concept, they proved to be too high off the ground for most average-sized riders to actually sit on, which rightly meant that the said committee had to go back to their drawing boards.

Perhaps it is best to draw a complete veil over all of BSA/Triumph's final 650 cc machines, not least because few of them were produced following those numerous enforced delays. Furthermore, the company that had conspired to kill the traditional Bonneville were £8 million in the red and nearly at the road's end.

Left above
Unit engine-to-gearbox construction arrived for 1963, which meant yet another new frame due to the later powerplant being physically shorter than its predecessor

Left below
Spotted at Daytona's Annual Speed Week during 1986, a pre-1970 Bonneville after receiving the full American treatment!

Above
The final pre-oil-in-frame 1970 Bonneville, arguably best of them all, and before anyone says anything, yes, I do know that this bike should have twin windtone horns

Racing again

Production racing featured high on the list of Bert Hopwood's and Doug Hele's priorities once the anti-racing Edward Turner moved his seat to BSA, and who better to spearhead their attack than their own works road tester Percy Tait, who also happened to be one of Britain's best road racers. His experience had already resulted in the twin-carburettor race kit which helped transform the old Tiger 110 used by Mike Hailwood and Dan Shorey to win 1958's Thruxton 500-miler which, incidentally, was the first such endurance race run in Britain.

Entries for the Thruxton event had been limited to supposedly standard production machines. Special race kits were allowable, however, provided they were already listed by each motorcycle's manufacturer as optional extras within their existing catalogues. Ironically, it was this very rule that ultimately caused the demise of this once very popular form of racing.

Right
With the Thruxton's fairing removed, one can just see the separate extra oil feeder pipe supplying the exhaust camshaft and tappets, a unique feature of all genuine T120R racers

Below
Classic racer Malcolm Clarke's genuine 1965 works-specification T120R production racing Bonnie, a truly superb, well-documented bike which, even in its own era, was rare in the extreme

Cheating by listing race goodies that, in fact were never generally available became rife, Triumph being no better than most. They built up a batch of outright works racers which they lent out through a few favoured dealers to top Grand Prix racing jockeys.

None of those machines could be bought by the man in the street unless, that is, his name happened to be something like Mike Hailwood or Geoff Duke! Catalogues and parts lists were often printed retrospectively and back-dated to get around race regulations.

Triumph built just over 70 of these special race bikes, and collectively they dominated the 1965, 1966 and 1967 Thruxton series, even filling most of the intermediate places. Percy Tait himself finished second in 1966 along with co-rider Phil Read after they had actually led for much of the way.

Geoff Duke provided John Hartle with one of these bikes to win 1967's first ever Production TT and similarly Malcolm Uphill shattered 1969's record by winning at a then quite staggering average race speed of 99.99 mph. This proved to be the Thruxton T120 limited-edition's swan-song, however.

From then onwards, Triumph concentrated on racing their triples in the up-to-750 cc class, whilst Percy Tait used a highly-tuned and phenomenally successful Tiger 100 for 500 cc racing. This led to Doug Hele building a small batch of 500 cc replicas for America's Daytona 200 series during 1966, with almost fairytale-like results.

Bud Elmore rode one and literally thrashed all comers, including the 750 cc works-entered Harleys. Furthermore, he raised the race record to a 96.58 mph average. As a result, Triumph hurriedly re-christened their twin-carburettor Tiger 100 model, which was about to be released, calling it the T100T Daytona in honour of Elmore's great victory.

Six even further developed machines were sent over for 1967's races, where Dick Hammer took the lead before he crashed and remounted, leaving Gary Nixon to win. Elmore, this time, came a close second, while Triumph's other bikes finished seventh, eighth and ninth, with Hammer more than a lap adrift in 15th place.

Not a genuine Thruxton, but a superbly-built replica, based on 1964's sports roadster Bonneville

Below

*Malcolm Uphill and his works-prepared
1967 Thruxton on the Isle of Man TT
circuit, where apart from winning in 1969,
he also became the first person to lap at
over 100 mph on a production machine
(100.37 mph)*

Off-road and on

Middle-aged spread, or rather full rear suspension, resulting in an over-long 55.75 in. wheelbase, put paid to the pre-unit Trophy as a serious off-road machine by the very late 1950s. This meant that Meriden no longer had a competitive twin on offer.

The picture wasn't all doom and gloom, however, for Triumph's works team was already winning again using converted unit-construction-engined roadsters the average wheelbase of which happened to be some 3 in. shorter. As a result, they were proving to be a far better basis than even the old Trophy.

Meriden would never again offer a competition works replica twin, but fortunately were more than happy to give advice and supply special parts to any private competitors who wished to convert a unit-construction roadster model. It was actually quite an easy conversion.

Below

Triumph works team trials star Roy Peplow campaigned this all-alloy-engined 500 throughout 1963–4, and still reckons it was the best bike he ever rode. Interestingly, it started life as a 1961 roadster taken back by the factory under guarantee as a rogue

Right

Number '316' is one of 1966's final factory-prepared International Six Days Trial team bikes. It was ridden by Gordon Farley that year to a gold medal in Sweden, whereas '318' was both built and ridden a year later by Roy Peplow, following the official works team's total disbandment

Overleaf

A closer look at '316' (registered HUE 256D) when it was in my ownership. Note the high-pressure CO_2 tyre inflator bottle and the ISDT scrutineers' green/maroon markings all over the machine. This is radioactive paint so that the event's organizers could run spot checks against cheating through component substitution simply by running a geiger counter over it. In this way, it could be checked even if the paint lay under inches of mud

Above

*Triumph's BSA-framed early 1970s
production Adventurer, or Trophy Trail
model as it also became known, was
advertised as incorporating the Group's
combined off-road experience. In truth,
though, it remained a very poor relation
to their pukka works bikes*

Triumph's official team long continued using the standard machine's steel
mudguards, fuel tank, dualseat, and most other heavy roadster components
well into the 1960s, winning far more ISDT medals in this period than any
other British manufacturer. This rather proves that they were on the right
lines.

Neither were those works engines particularly exotic. The 650s employed
the police Saint model's basic tune, including a hot inlet but soft exhaust cam,
single, but larger-bore carburettor, and exactly the same wider-ratio gear set as
used by the 'boys in blue' for walking-pace riding when on such duties as
Royal escort.

The 350s and 500s were to the coming Daytona engine's tune, but again
with a larger single carburettor and the 5TA's softer exhaust camshaft,
coupled to that bike's shallow-radius tappet followers (which further altered
the valve timing). Finally, their wider-ratio gear set was the one listed for one-
day trialing.

Perhaps most ironic of all was that these stock-chassis machines actually
handled better off-road than on. This was because Triumph were still using
Edward Turner's steep steering head angle that was not exactly known for

Above

The 1972 on/off-road Trailblazer 250SS similarly used a BSA Victor scrambler-type frame, but beyond that, its only claim to fame was for pose value

good roadholding, whereas the upright front fork stance suited the competition bikes to perfection.

Most successful of all were the 350s and 500s, largely because they were physically smaller and, therefore, much easier to ride. This is why Triumph overbored some 500s to 501 cc for running in the larger 750 capacity class, as happened in 1966 for the ISDT in Sweden (the last that Meriden were officially involved in).

Britain's Trophy team was chosen as usual that year by the Auto Cycle Union and comprised Triumph's Ray Sayer with John Giles on 350s alongside Roy Peplow and Sammy Miller on 500s. Ken Heanes rode one of the overbored 500s in the 750 class rather than a genuine 650. Similarly, Gordon Farley rode a 'works' 501 cc in the No. 2 (Vase) Squad. The Lampkin brothers, who were BSA's top two works riders, likewise used Triumph power, although housed in adapted versions of that company's Victor Scrambler frames, Arthur completing the Trophy Squad and Alan the Vase.

All gained gold medals, so Triumph won what was the last of their many Manufacturer's awards, but Britain's Trophy Team as a whole was very narrowly beaten into second berth by the East Germans. Messrs Heanes and Sayer had

Right
A 750 cc Tiger Trail, first built during the early 1980s to meet the demand of the Co-operative's French market. Very nice it was, too, as a dual-purpose trail bike

each lost 20 marks early on, then Giles and Lampkin both dropped another 20 for clocking in early at a control point.

As to the actual basis of these final works ISDT machines, they were merely a small batch of American export-specification Tiger 100Cs which had been taken off the production line for refettling by Henry Vale and his lads in Triumph's competition shop. This meant lightening them generally and, of course, reassembling them with extra care.

Very few Tiger 100Cs ever reached the home market, which was a great pity, for they were quite the nearest thing to Triumph's works bikes, with the exception of a few heavy bits, like steel fuel tanks and mudguards. The later 1972–3 BSA rather than Triumph-inspired Adventurer/Trophy trail model, on the other hand, remains but a poor relation.

Above

Substitute an alloy fuel tank, single saddle, smaller front brake and trials tyres, and this American-specification Tiger 100C would virtually assume works ISDT team bike status, for it was already supplied with wide-ratio gears and the correct state of engine tune

Much delayed triples

Anticipation, it is said, can occasionally be better than fulfilment, and so it was with the BSA/Triumph Group's November 1968-onwards triples. These had been hinted at, and even occasionally glimpsed in prototype form for a surprising number of years.

The story begins in 1961 when Bert Hopwood was asked by BSA/Triumph's main board to consider enlarging the Bonneville's engine capacity to 750 cc. He opined that this was too large for a vertical twin, that it would be unbalanced and would suffer from unacceptable levels of vibration.

He and Doug Hele countered by suggesting that instead they add a third cylinder to the smaller 498 cc Daytona engine to increase its capacity to almost the required 750 cc. This would result in a cylinder firing every 120 degrees which, in turn, would virtually cancel out any untoward vibration.

Below
Triumph's Mk 1 Trident T150, exactly as it was marketed for 1969

Above

*A single disc instead of drum brake, new
front forks and arguably a much nicer
colour scheme, identifies this bike as a
T150 Mk 2*

Bench tests of the prototype proved this immediately, and it also gave a massive 58 bhp at 7250 rpm, which was a full 12 bhp more than a well-sorted Bonneville Then they set off for track testing at Lindley, where it was spotted and reported, wrongly, as a three-cylinder Bonneville.

The only remaining mystery is why on earth it was so long before this bike entered production, especially as Hopwood himself claims that there were never any significant development problems and that he could have been marketing it in 1963. For some reason BSA's board steadfastly refused to give the go-ahead.

We may never know why BSA held off for almost five years, but their indecision certainly cost them dear, for, when they did come, these fabulous performance bikes only enjoyed a brief period of popularity before Honda stole most of their thunder with even more exotic 750 cc fours.

If that was not bad enough, BSA also increasingly saddled this entirely Triumph-developed design with their own ever more garish styling, although Meriden's men scored an occasional point in retaliation, such as with their famous, and aptly nicknamed, 'Slippery Sam' racing Trident. This made a habit of thrashing its BSA-badged opponents.

Rumour had it that Norton-Villiers only 'rescued' BSA Triumph because they wanted those magnificent three-cylinder engines and the Wankel patents. Subsequent history suggests that, indeed, this may have been true, so the final T160 electric-start jobs were actually NVT-inspired, but looked more like true Triumphs.

Right
Triumph tester and works team road racer Percy Tait cracking along at a goodly rate of knots on one of the factory's famous racing triples at Donington

Overleaf
A real grudge match this, with Percy Tait riding 'Slippery Sam' at Brands Hatch, trying to stay ahead of BSA's John 'Mooneyes' Cooper with Allan Barnett running third. Being a dyed-in-the-wool Triumph man, Percy wouldn't want Small Heath's rival triple to get ahead

Left

Almost 20 years on and Triumph's triples are still racing (and winning), not just in classic events either, for this picture was taken in 1989 and shows Dave Pither and his T150 approaching Signpost Corner in the Isle of Man's full International TT

Right
What might have been, given a little more time and money. Doug Hele and Bert Hopwood's final and very exciting four-cylinder prototype, which was scuppered by BSA/Triumph's demise

Left

New owners Norton-Villiers-Triumph breathed fresh life into the mid-1970s triple by mating a BSA inclined-forward-type engine to a development of Triumph's chassis and adding electric start. I once bought such a Triumph T160 and loved it

Right

Californian Craig Vetter conducted a futuristic T160 restyling exercise for the American market. However, his forward-mounted footrests, skimpy seat, high handlebars and minute-capacity fuel tank meant that the resulting X75 was high on pose value, but very tiring to ride

End of the road?

BSA/Triumph's caretaker board fought on valiantly through 1972 in the hope of bringing this once great company back from the brink of disaster. They took some pretty strong measures, including making large-scale redundancies at all levels, while also raising more instant capital by selling spares and completed stocks at virtually give-away prices.

The master plan was to shrink the company sufficiently to be able to move BSA's production in with Triumph's at Meriden, then sell off Small Heath along with most of the combined companies' various other assets. This might have saved them, but for a cruel stroke of fate.

Ray Pickrell, meanwhile, had won June 1972's Isle of Man Production TT for Triumph at a new record average of 104.23 mph, and Bert Hopwood was quietly working on redesigning, strengthening and enlarging the Bonneville's engine to nearer 750 cc, despite his earlier misgivings. For a while, it even seemed as if Meriden might come out of 1972 showing a small profit.

Then fate struck, with the almighty dollar being devalued and, in conseqence, sterling interest rates rapidly rising. As a result, £300,000 was wiped off the value of monies due for export machines sold.

The only options left were either to file for bankruptcy, or urgently request the Department of Trade and Industry (DTI) for a government loan. Although the DTI were agreeable, they added a pre-condition that BSA/Triumph must first merge with Norton-Villiers, assuming, of course, that the latter would have them.

Merger talks were still going on in 1973 when Hopwood unveiled the long-awaited Bonneville 750. However, it was actually only of 724 cc capacity, for there had been no money available for commissioning new cylinder castings, and insufficient meat left in the old ones for boring them out to a full 750.

Norton-Villiers eventually accepted £4.9 million of taxpayers' money to take the ailing BSA/Triumph Group under their wing and, in consequence, became Norton-Villiers-Triumph (NVT), but then Dennis Poore, their Chairman, announced that his plan was to close down Meriden rather than Small Heath.

This all happened during September 1973, just when Triumph managed to afford the casting of new cylinder barrels that would transform the new Bonneville into its intended 747 cc. It would be years, however, before many of them reached the market, for on hearing the closure plan, Meriden's workers promptly commenced their factory's long-running blockade.

Mick Grant took Triumph's famous 'Slippery Sam' three-cylinder racer to its fourth consecutive TT victory during June 1974, as production of Tridents gradually resumed at Small Heath. However, there would not be any more twins built until the previously mentioned impasse had been solved.

Above
First of the Limited Editions, one of a 1000 especially-finished Bonnevilles, all built during 1977 to commemorate Queen Elizabeth's Silver Jubilee. Nice bikes they were, too, but aimed very much towards the collectors' market

Above

The 1979–80 Limited Edition Executive models were far better finished than the Jubilees and came ready fitted with a very comfortable 'King and Queen' seat, a nose-cone fairing, and superbly-made Sigma luggage boxes, all colour coded

Overleaf

One could order a 750 cc Triumph in any parts-bin specification during the early 1980s, for the Co-operative were in deep financial trouble by then and desperately needed the money. Ironically, this resulted in some of the nicest bikes ever made, including this Lester magnesium-wheeled Bonneville Special

Compromise was finally reached during March 1975, when NVT who were under pressure from Britain's government, agreed to hand Triumph's factory and trade mark to a newly-formed Meriden Workers Co-operative who, incidentally, were to receive a £4.2 million starter loan from public funds.

NVT retained the Triumph triple's name and manufacturing rights, so were responsible for the electric-start T160s introduced that year. The Meriden Co-operative, on the other hand, abandoned any hope of ever resuming production of the smaller twins in favour of concentrating on the 1973-conceived, but still as yet unmarketed, 747 cc larger-capacity Bonneville.

Maybe a one-engine-based range was a far cry from Triumph's previous glories, but those new 750s soon found a worthwhile niche in the market, not least because they were well engineered, reasonably quick, handled superbly and remained simple to work on. Thus, they possessed a certain, not inconsiderable, 'olde worlde' charm.

Few riders of other marques could even hope to stay within sight of a 750 Bonneville that was well ridden over a tight, twisting road (then or now), although the engine's vibes do begin to become unpleasant at constant speeds in excess of 70 mph. Up to that figure, however, they can best be compared with BMW's Boxer, but have very superior handling.

Electronic ignition greatly helps to smooth out the vibes, and indeed it became a standard fitment for 1980, whereas electric-start arrived with 1981's full luggage-equipped Executive model. However, this was not standard to all other versions, and certainly was not necessary, for few big bikes have ever been easier to kick start.

One really exciting version should have been the TSS eight-valver, not least because the super-fast prototype beat everything else in sight during 1982's Daytona Battle of Twins race. Unfortunately, its hoped for sales were torpedoed by an outside supplier who lumbered Triumph with porous cylinder and cylinder head castings.

Meriden lost a fortune in guarantee claims on that one which, in turn, set back production of their new, ironically titled Phoenix range. This would have enjoyed very advanced design 650, 750 and 900 cc water-cooled dohc engines had the Co-operative not crashed instead of rising phoenix-like from the ashes of the TSS.

Enfield India bid the Official Receiver £55,000 for Triumph's name and manufacturing rights and thought they would be successful, but the surprise winner turned out to be a millionaire builder named John Bloor. He sub-let Bonneville production to Les Harris of Devon (finished in 1988), while continuing himself with the Phoenix development which, at the time of writing had a hoped-for 1990 production date.

Left

The eight-valve TSS was closely based on this bike, used by Joe Minoto to beat Japan's and Italy's entire motorcycle might in 1982's Daytona Battle of Twins race. It should have been a real winner, too, had it not been let down by porous castings, stemming from outside suppliers

Above

*Largely intended for police use, the
rubber-mounted TSS-engined T58-1 of
1983. With this, it was hoped to finally
end vibration problems, always
Triumph's biggest bogey with the 750s*

Had the mid-1980s media ever seen this one, they would have had a real field day! This picture, commissioned secretly by the almost moneyless Triumph Co-operative, was taken when they were seriously looking into ways of taking over the already bankrupt Hesketh concern! Quite incredible to even contemplate really